Why do I feel so distant from God?

Paul LeBoutillier

Copyright © 2024 by Paul D. LeBoutillier

All rights reserved.

Unless otherwise noted, Scripture quotations are from The ESV® Bible (The Holy Bible, English Standard Version®), © 2001 by Crossway, a publishing ministry of Good News Publishers. Used by permission. All rights reserved."

Scripture quotations marked NIV84 are taken from the Holy Bible, New International Version®, NIV®. Copyright ©1973, 1978, 1984 by Biblica, Inc.™ Used by permission of Zondervan. All rights reserved worldwide. www.zondervan.com The "NIV" and "New International Version" are trademarks registered in the United States Patent and Trademark Office by Biblica, Inc.™

No portion of this book may be reproduced in any form without written permission from the publisher or author, except as permitted by U.S. copyright law.

Cover design and interior layout by Nellie Coleman

To my wife and partner in ministry. How can I begin to thank you for your tireless encouragement and help in both writing, proofing and organizing this little booklet and all during a time when you are enduring your own set of trials. You inspire me.

To my oldest daughter who edited this work and put up with my constant manuscript changes while showing me the Lord's own patience and understanding.

And to all the saints who wrote to me over the past several years, making this pastor more aware of the daily challenges facing believers as they walk out their faith...

...this book is humbly dedicated.

Paul LeBoutillier

November 2024

Contents

Foreword	VI
1. Why do you feel so distant from God?	1
2. Because you've lost the confidence of your salvation	6
3. Because your relationship with God is based on performance	16
4. Because the enemy has convinced you of things that aren't true	30
5. Because living in a broken world has shaken your faith	40
6. A Final Word	52
About the author	56

Foreword

The year was 1991.

As a young girl of seven, I was growing up in rural eastern Oregon with my younger brother and parents. The only thing that separated our simple family home from the widespread onion fields was a road called Butler Boulevard where onion trucks would lumber up and down daily and sometimes drop, you guessed it, onions.

It was alongside Butler Boulevard that I often walked the one block between our home and the church where my dad was the pastor. I loved to get up extra early on Sunday mornings hoping I could walk with Dad when he was ready to head to the church.

Those early years held comforting routines, simple patterns. The church was small in numbers and my parents did what most church planters do — pretty much everything. Dad normally straightened every chair once we'd turned the lights on and unlocked the doors. It was his quiet time to think through his teaching for the morning. The paper bulletins would be folded and set out, the old overhead projector turned on so it could 'warm up' in time.

At the age of seven, I hadn't any notion of what God was setting into motion and would ultimately bring about through my parents' faithfulness to follow a calling on their lives, a calling to pastor and serve and minister to people in the eastern Oregon/western Idaho area for 34 years now.

That little church fellowship in Ontario, Oregon grew. It became home to hundreds and hundreds of believers over the years. With the creation of the Internet and YouTube, my dad's weekly verse by verse teachings were eventually posted and found by thousands upon thousands. He quickly became a pastor to many around the world who were searching for the truth and peace that comes from God's Word, taught in a way that was simple and easy to understand. The constant emails and letters my parents receive today from online viewers are daily reminders of all that the Lord had planned from the beginning, all that would come from an imperfect but faithful Bible teacher who was first called to a small church on an onion truck road in Oregon.

Fast-forward to today. You're about to read a book written by my Dad — my walking partner in the 90's on Butler Boulevard. A man with unique insight at this stage in life, who has been ministering to Christians both local and around the world, answering their Bible questions and praying with them through the pains of life for almost 40 years. His storehouse of wisdom is immense. Just as helpful is the collection of what those years of ministry have taught him and what has been summarized in this book: the common ways many believers struggle in their faith and how they can rebuild and restore their intimacy with God by knowing and applying the Word.

I hope you take heart from the chapters that follow. You'll get to read some of the letters Dad has received over the years and perhaps you'll see some of your own struggles in the words written and the answers given. Either way, I hope you'll be blessed. I was honored to play a small role in helping Dad bring this book to print.

Nellie (LeBoutillier) Coleman

Chapter 1
Why do you feel so distant from God?

"Why, O LORD, do you stand far away?" Psalm 10:1

I've always loved the honest and raw voice of the Psalmist as quoted above. It's a cry that I'm sure we all can relate to. This is confirmed by search engines, showing that people are "googling" questions like:

- *Why do I feel so distanced from God?*

- *What to do when you feel God is distant?*

- *Why do we feel disconnected from God?*

- *What does the Bible say about feeling distant from God?*

Over the past several years I've had the rather unique opportunity to hear from believers from all over the world about the challenges they face in their relationship with God. Despite the cultural differences that exist, the problems and pitfalls of life that cause Christians to feel a distance in their relationship to God are amazingly similar. The solutions are even more so.

Let me be quick to add that I make no claims in this short book to cover every possible cause for feelings of distance from God. I'm not even sure I know them all. But what I *do* know is that it can happen quickly and seemingly without warning. All it takes is an almost unconscious setting aside of certain key truths from God's Word. When that happens, believers quickly find themselves in a fog of confusion and ultimately vulnerable to the suggestions of the enemy.

My goal in this book is to expose some common areas most often communicated to me by others and experienced by myself where we can easily let go of God's truth in favor of believing a lie.

Don't laugh, but as a Pastor, I've always seen myself as a kind of spiritual chiropractor. Instead of adjusting someone's spine or neck, I offer truth adjustments from the Bible. This is needful because just as a person's skeletal frame can get out of whack, causing all kinds of pain and discomfort, so also our spiritual lives can become just as misaligned and painful.

When that happens, people need a "truth adjustment" — an infusion of living truth, unfiltered with no apologies — the power of which can break the hold of the enemy fostered by faulty thinking. The wonderful result is that grasping such living truth can almost instantly restore a closeness with God. As Jesus said, *"...**you will know the truth, and the truth will set you free.**" (John 8:32)*

In the coming chapters I want to highlight some common reasons believers find themselves feeling distant from God.

Chapter Two will focus on those whose feelings of distance from God are the result of doubting their salvation.

Chapter Three will address believers who have a gravitational pull toward legalism and a performance-based approach to knowing and pleasing God.

Chapter Four will investigate the challenges of those who seem to be engaged in constant spiritual warfare and because of their weariness, feel distant from God.

Chapter Five will deal with how believers often react to living in a world that is so irreparably broken with its unrelenting challenges and how the frustration and disappointments in life can cause us to feel distanced from God.

And in the final chapter, I hope to leave you with a word of encouragement that will help you press on each and every day in the knowledge of God's never-ending presence in your life.

One final thought before we get started...

This book is primarily written for believers who have once been close to the Lord but, for whatever reason, now feel a distance from Him and want to know how that closeness and intimacy can be restored. I am aware, however, that someone reading this book may have *never* felt close to God at any time in your life. So, before I go any further, I need to let you know about a different sort of reason people will feel a separation from God.

The fact is, we all begin our lives separated and distanced from God. This is the result of what is known biblically as the fall of mankind recorded for us in the book of Genesis. There the Bible recounts the beginning of all things, including the first eruption of "sin" — defined in the original languages as "missing the mark." Since that first occurrence of sin, all mankind has henceforth been born into the same broken and fallen condition that is marked by a profound separation from God.

The Good News is that God has bridged that separation through the finished work of Jesus on the cross. If we will simply respond to Him by faith and trust fully in the sacrifice of Jesus, who willingly bore for us the penalty of our sin, that spiritual and otherwise eternal separation from God can be instantly removed.

If you have never confessed your sin and put your faith in Jesus Christ for the forgiveness of sins, I strongly encourage you to do that before reading any further. All it takes is a simple prayer of faith that goes something like this:

"Lord, I come to You painfully aware of the sin that has caused me to be estranged from You, but I come now, confessing the darkness of my heart and asking You to wash me clean. I believe that Jesus died on the cross for my sin and I accept His death on my behalf. I humbly ask You to fill me with Your Holy Spirit and teach me how to live my life for You. I ask all this in the mighty name of the One who gave His life that I might be forgiven and rose again that I might live — Jesus my Savior. Amen!"

If you prayed that prayer, I want you to know that God heard you and the Bible says that you are now a child of God. I want to encourage you to do a complete study through the New Testament book of John. You'll find some links here:

Read the book of John at: **esv.org/John+1/** or take a photo of the code below

Listen to my study through the book of John at: **lifebibleministry.com/john** or take a photo of the code below.

Chapter 2
Because you've lost the confidence of your salvation

> *"Now I would remind you, brothers, of the gospel I preached to you, which you received, in which you stand, and by which you are being saved..."*
> **1 Corinthians 15:1-2**

I have a memory of the very time I first embraced the Gospel of Jesus Christ. I was about fifteen years old and had heard the real message of the cross for the very first time. The telling of it had rattled me to my soul and made me aware of just how deeply my Redeemer had suffered on my behalf. The next day and I found myself sitting on the floor of my bedroom, contemplating all that I had heard the night before. In a moment of time I recall offering up a simple prayer and saying, "Yes,

Lord. I accept!" At that very moment a burst of sunshine fell upon me from a nearby window and I felt the presence of the Lord in a way I had never experienced before.

From that day until now — more than 50 years later — I have never once doubted the assurance of my salvation, nor have I questioned God's love for me. But as a pastor I have learned that my own situation is not the norm. The letter that follows is one of many sharing a similar experience.

Dear Pastor Paul,

Please allow me to apologize ahead of time for how long this is, but I felt you needed a little background to understand my situation.

I came to Christ in my early childhood and I attended church every Sunday with my family. I progressed in my understanding of God's Word to the degree that at the age of 15 I was allowed to teach a Sunday School class for the five and six year olds. I really loved sharing Bible stories with those kids each week. I, myself, loved the Word of God and I've always been comforted in the knowledge that Jesus paid my penalty by dying for me on the cross. I've never been ashamed of Jesus or anything that He has done for me.

When I graduated from high school things began to change for me. I moved out of my parent's home and relocated to a city where jobs were easier to come by. Eventually I found a good position working as a receptionist for a dental office. During that time I did my best to attend church but, I guess life just got busy and as time went on I found myself staying home for the weekend in favor of getting things done around my apartment. I would inevitably feel guilty and promise the Lord I would attend the following week but I rarely followed through. Each week seemed to produce a new flurry of activity and before long I just settled into a routine of making it to church every 4 to 6 weeks.

I'm ashamed to say I eventually became satisfied with that kind of a commitment.

After I had been at the dental office for a few months I started seeing a man named Carl. He was one of our suppliers who popped in every couple of weeks to drop off supplies. I guess he kind of swept me off my feet because within a year of taking that job I found myself married and moving into a home with my new husband. Within the first year of our marriage Carl and I had a daughter.

Carl had been raised in a home where God, the Bible and church attendance were pretty much ignored and it wasn't long before I found myself neglecting church attendance completely. I tried talking to Carl about God and the Bible but he is very adept at explaining why he doesn't believe such things. I'm ashamed to say that I have been unable to defend my faith. In some cases, I've even begun to see his point of view, which only causes me to doubt everything I've ever learned.

We've since had another baby and I guess you could say we are a reasonably happy family but I have to confess I occasionally feel waves of guilt about my faith. Both of my parents are still active in their church and every time I talk to them on the phone I feel such guilt about neglecting the faith they raised me to cherish. The joy that I once had has been missing for a long time now.

Last week, while I was picking up a few things from the grocery store, I ran into a former co-worker from the dental office. She ended up inviting Carl and me to come to church with them some weekend. I told her I would talk to Carl about it but I knew in my heart he would never agree to go. I think she saw in my expression that there wasn't much hope in us coming to church because she went on to tell me about your teachings on YouTube. She encouraged me to listen during the day while I'm working around the house. I've been doing that for a while now and I have to tell you, it feels so incredible to hear the Word of God again! I really love it, but I have to confess that there are times I wonder if God wants me back. I mean, didn't I abandon my faith? I even wonder if heaven is a possibility for me anymore?

These thoughts and doubts have shaken me to the core and even keep me up at night. Do you have any words of encouragement?

Britney

***

As I've said previously, Britney's testimony is not at all uncommon. Although she started off well, Britney allowed a distance to come between her and everything Christ-centered and it lasted so long that the truth of God's Word became a faint echo in her heart. Where she once enjoyed security and joy concerning her salvation, she now wrestled with doubt and fear. What a horrible thing it is for a believer to wake up one day and find that they've drifted far away from the security of knowing who they are in Jesus.

Every follower of Jesus needs to know and understand that the enemy of your soul wants, more than anything, to bring you to a place of confusion and doubt concerning your salvation. He does this because doubt is the opposite of faith, and Satan knows that, if you are willing to entertain doubt, he can easily get you in a spiritual headlock. From there it is an easy thing for him to wrestle you to the ground and pin your shoulders to the mat.

I have said for many years that when a believer foolishly falls to these attacks and begins to question their salvation, they will quickly find themselves in the playground of the enemy. The power of Satan to breed hopelessness is based on his ability to fill your perspective with nothing but feelings of failure and shame. From there, he will relentlessly beat you over the head with your past until the cross of Christ is completely out of sight.

> **"Whoever believes that he lost his salvation today because he has sinned, believes he had it yesterday because he was good."**
>
> — **Martyn Lloyd-Jones**

Satan knows full well that the cross of Jesus is *the answer* to the weary, doubting soul. And the *last* thing he wants is for that once strong believer to rediscover the power of that cross through the Word of God.

Understanding the Keys to Satan's Attacks

The power of Satan to get your eyes off your Savior and His finished work on the cross lies in one of mankind's biggest weaknesses — the strong gravitational pull in all of us to fixate on *self*. To say that we are all self-centered is an understatement. The Bible tells us our hearts are *"deceitful above all things, and desperately sick..." (Jeremiah 17:9)* and we would do well to believe it. Mankind's propensity to become entirely centered on anything that is self-serving or self-satisfying knows no bounds.

In other words, we are deeply selfish people even while being quite unwilling to admit it. Satan knows this and exploits our weakness for his own ends.

The enemy crouches in the tall grass waiting patiently for the believer to either wander off from the safety of fellowship with Jesus or to stumble morally and he springs his attack, beginning his work of chipping away at their security. His aim is to slowly turn their eyes away from Jesus and onto all they have done wrong until that is all they can see.

The believer must resist the temptation, however strong, to focus on *self* and turn his or her gaze back to the cross. ***This is accomplished by turning to the Word of God and allowing it to cleanse and renew our badly discouraged heart***.

Grace Triumphs Over Failure

Satan knows that failure has a powerful way of shifting an otherwise healthy believer's focus from God to self. And even though this person at one time believed with all their heart that salvation is and always has been a free gift of God's love, their intense failures can easily turn them sideways until they start to wonder if somehow their actions have nullified their ability to be loved or saved.

> "God *will* forgive and promises to cleanse us from *all* unrighteousness"

I've gotten emails from people who were so focused on their own pitiful failures and moral brokenness that, but for the grace of God, they were unable to hear the truth any longer. All might be lost were it not for the immense power of the Word of God to break the chains of the enemy!

To the heart that is weighed down with the failures and brokenness of self so that the cross is no longer in view, I share the power of the following words:

> *"For by grace you have been saved through faith. And this is not your own doing; it is the gift of God, not a result of works, so that no one may boast." Ephesians 2:8-9*

This single passage from Ephesians is *so* powerful because it reminds us of many things:

- We are saved by **grace** — *apart from anything we can do to earn it.*

- We are saved **through faith** — by believing that Jesus died on the cross for us,

- The **sacrifice of Jesus was *enough*** to secure our eternal forgiveness.

Here's the conclusion: Salvation is a gift! It cannot be earned through moral goodness and cannot be lost through moral failure.

What a blast of living truth this is for the wounded heart! To keep Ephesians 2:8-9 front and center is to stay connected and close to the Lord; safe from attacks of doubt as well as a host of false ideas. You'll be able to say, *'No! That's wrong. It is by grace that I am saved through faith — period!'*

It is truly amazing how a simple, yet powerful blast of truth can radically transform a heart from isolation and doubt to assurance and fellowship with God. It's the truth that every wandering heart needs to hear — God *will* forgive me and promises to cleanse me from *all unrighteousness.*

Please be aware, dear child of God, that the enemy will be quick to challenge God's promise with plenty of accusations and condemnation. He will declare such a thing to be patently impossible. It is at this point that the believer must bravely don the shield of faith and resist the temptation to doubt God's Word. As James exhorted us: ***resist the devil and he will flee from you. (James 4:7)***

The Story Continues...

Britney's story, like yours, is yet to be completed. After recognizing the distance in her relationship with Jesus, her greatest need was to return to the Lord in confession and to reacquaint her heart with the sacrifice that Jesus made for her on the cross. She must surrender her failures there and allow them all to be nailed to the cross of Christ. This is always the toughest step for people like Britney — to surrender one's biggest failures and personal disappointments and to leave them nailed to the cross.

The Apostle Paul reminds us in 2 Timothy 2:13 that *"...**if we are faithless, he remains faithful...**"* This isn't an excuse to fail but rather serves to remind us that the Lord Jesus understands our human weaknesses and failings and desires that we would lay those things at His feet. God's love for us has never been dependent on our ability to live mistake free, but instead has always been grounded in His own boundless love.

My dear sister, Britney, and I call you "sister" because that is what you are in Christ. The enemy is trying desperately to get you to believe something that is untrue — that the path back to your Lord is no longer open to you and that everything you once held dear can never be yours again. But as Jesus told you, Satan is a liar and the father of lies (John 8:44), whereas your heavenly Father is a God of truth. And His truth will set you free. Let me tell you what is true:

> **"If we confess our sins, he is faithful and just to forgive us our sins and cleanse us from all unrighteousness." 1 John 1:9 ESV**

Let this be the day that you confess your distance from God. Lay it all at the foot of the cross. And, as you do, know deep in your heart that your Father will forgive you and cleanse you. This is His firm promise to you as revealed in the passage above. Take this promise and make it yours.

Pray for your husband every day and trust the Lord to move upon his heart. Pray also for your children and get back into fellowship without delay. Be in the Word daily and take hold of everything that God has given to you. Hold it tightly and refuse to let go. Take one day at a time and trust the Lord to help you move forward. He is faithful.

God bless you.

Chapter 3
Because your relationship with God is based on performance

"For all who rely on works of the law are under a curse..." *Galatians 3:10*

"...you are not under law but under grace."
Romans 6:14

> "...whoever has entered God's rest has also rested from his works as God did from his." *Hebrews 4:10*

The Roots of Legalism

If you search in the Bible for the words *legalism* or *legalistic* you won't find them anywhere. And yet, the phenomenon of strict rule-keeping is sprinkled throughout the biblical text and nowhere more clearly than in the New Testament.

During His earthly ministry Jesus repeatedly butted heads with the religious legalists of Israel and the Apostle Paul seemed to be constantly warring with those who insisted the path to God was wrought through personal effort and the keeping of strict rules.

It's amazing to me that legalism still exists today with the message of the Bible so abundantly clear on the subject. The futility of approaching God on the basis of personal merit is obvious in the pages of Scripture. Yet there remains a devoted segment of the population that is both eager and receptive to the message that legalism conveys.

I've come to understand that certain personalities have a natural gravitational pull toward keeping rules. Many of them, I find, are aware of this tendency and have no problem with it. There are others, however, who had legalism thrust upon them in their formative years in a home or environment that functioned according to strict adherence to rules and regulations. Regardless of whether they ever learned to enjoy them, rule-keeping has now become imprinted on their hearts.

It is these two types of individuals who typically struggle the most when attempting to navigate their walk with God, especially in the area of trying to figure out where the Old Testament laws fit into their Christian faith. This is all the more difficult for those who've had the unfortunate experience of being influenced by a Bible teacher or mentor who emphasized rule-keeping as a way of approaching God.

The keeping of rules may offer a modicum of comfort for some but there are good reasons why that kind of lifestyle stands in clear contradiction to the life of faith believers are called to live. Legalism will *never* help you feel close to God. In fact, it will do the opposite.

Dear Pastor Paul,

I was raised in a denominational church and, to be quite honest, I never heard much about what it meant to be saved until after I graduated and moved away from home. One day I got an invitation in the mail to attend a seminar that promised to highlight and explain what the Bible has to say about the end times. I was intrigued so I decided to attend.

The presentation was really well done and I was hooked. I started attending the church that was sponsoring the meeting and I've been going pretty regularly for the past three years. I have to tell you, I was really attracted to their message because they basically laid out what I have to do to go to heaven and I've always been a sucker for checking off boxes. Rules make me feel safe.

This past January I got to know one of my co-workers (Julie) who is a Christian although she attends a different church in town. We've been talking a lot about the Bible and if I'm being honest, one of the things I find fascinating about her is her attitude — she's just so incredibly joyful! She has a confidence in her relationship with the Lord that I have to confess, I'm not sure I have.

As much as I like talking to Julie, this whole situation has created a crisis of faith for me. I'm concerned that the assurance of my salvation has been founded on keeping a certain day of the week and on all kinds of rules instead of on Jesus and what He did on the cross. I'm starting to doubt if I'm really saved! Can you help clear up the mess in my head??

Josh

***

Several years ago I was painting houses with a friend of mine and toward the end of the work day he would come to me and say, "What do you lack?" He was simply asking me what I had left to accomplish, but I recall the first time he said it I was unclear about what he was asking. I must've looked at him like he was speaking a foreign language, so he repeated the question, "What do you lack?" By this time he could tell I was totally confused, so he finally said, "What do you have left to finish?"

I got to thinking about that question in the ensuing years because, if there's one thing the Lord has made clear to me in that time, it is what I lack. And believe me, it's a lot! Yet, understanding one's lack is the starting point to both grasping and laying hold of God's grace. If we don't learn to depend upon God's grace, we will ultimately look to ourselves and our own abilities and efforts. Therein lies the root of legalism.

A Biblical Example

There is a fascinating account recorded in the Gospel of Matthew where Jesus was approached by a young man with a very revealing question. He came to Jesus and said, *"Teacher, what good deed must I do to have eternal life?" (Matthew 19:16)*

It seems like a straightforward question, yet it also reveals a popular belief among many in the world today. **What must I do to impress God so that He will accept me and allow me into heaven?**

Jesus responded to the young man saying, *"Why do you ask me about what is good? There is only one who is good." (Matthew 19:17)* Have you ever really stopped and thought about what Jesus said here? — because I can tell you confidently that the young man wasn't listening at all. If he had been, the conversation would have stopped right here.

Think about it — the young man asked what good deed was required of him to have eternal life. Jesus replied that there is only one who is good — referring to God. In other words, Jesus was telling the young man that He wasn't good, therefore attempting to produce "good deeds" was a futile idea!

But, as I said earlier, the young man completely missed the reality of our Lord's words, which is why Jesus had to go on to show him the utter futility of his goal of pleasing God through good works. Jesus began to list specific commandments given by God, such as, *"You shall not murder...You shall not commit adultery...You shall not steal...You shall not bear false witness... Honor your father and mother, and, You shall love your neighbor as yourself." (Exodus 20)*

I want to stop here to remind you that Peter referred to these commandments as *"...a yoke...that neither our fathers nor we have been able to bear?" (Acts 15:10)* Now please understand, Peter wasn't calling the Law itself an unbearable yoke. What was unbearable was the belief that *one must keep the Law and all the commandments as a requirement for salvation.*

So, while Peter called this idea an unbearable yoke, I want you now to hear how this young man viewed the keeping of these commands:

The young man said to Jesus, **"All these I have kept."**

Did you catch that? This young man looked into the face of the Perfect Son of God — the *only One who was good* — and he unabashedly claimed to have perfectly kept all those laws.

Now, if I were talking to someone living in that kind of self-deception, I would probably respond by saying, "Seriously? Are you *that* deluded??"

But Jesus is gentle and kind. He simply chose one of the commandments — **You shall love your neighbor as yourself** — and put the young man's claim to the test, saying, **"If you would be perfect, go, sell what you possess and give to the poor, and you will have treasure in heaven; and come, follow me." (Matthew 19:21)**

This was the perfect response. The young man had convinced himself that his ability to love his neighbor was in keeping with God's holy requirements. But when Jesus challenged him to show that kind of love by selling his possessions and donating the money to the poor, the man "**went away sorrowful, for he had great possessions.**"

The lesson here is both powerful and sobering. Mankind's capacity for self-deception is such that he can convince himself that he is up to the task of actually pleasing God through self-effort — even though God has made it clear that our best acts of righteousness (or goodness) are likened to "filthy rags" alongside His own utter purity and holiness.

Understanding our Relationship to the Law

Why do people become legalistic? Whether we know it or not, every man and woman has an inborn desire to please God and be accepted in His sight. And yet, sin has twisted our understanding of how to achieve that goal and we seek to obtain God's approval through our own self effort.

Arguably one of the most challenging areas, especially for new believers, has to do with how to interpret and apply the laws found in the Old Testament. Whole denominations have sprung up based on a fundamental misunderstanding and misinterpretation of how the New Testament believer ought to view and respond to the Old Testament Law.

When we speak of the Law, we're referring to that which God gave to Israel through Moses. This includes, but is not limited to, the Ten Commandments.

A new believer in Christ learns that the Bible is the Word of God, so, they read through the Old Testament and find that it contains many rules which cause them to wonder how all those regulations might apply to their life. To make the issue even more confusing, there are plenty of Bible teachers just waiting to mislead these new babes in Christ with teachings that fail to take in the biblical big picture.

This issue has been an ongoing challenge for many years. Essentially what Christians struggle with as it relates to the Law of Moses is how they can possibly harmonize it all with what they know to be the gospel of grace. To be frank, the difficulty of understanding the Law is one of the reasons a good number of believers feel safer studying the New Testament and rarely delve into the Old.

A question I hear quite often is, *"Are you saying the Ten Commandments are no longer important?"* — and the answer is, **of course they're important**. But, as the Apostle Paul stated, "**...*we know that the law is good, if one uses it properly." (1 Timothy 1:8 NIV84)***

Therein lies the problem. There's a whole lot of improper use of the Law going on today.

There are several passages I share with people along the lines of understanding how the Law of Moses applies to their lives and avoiding the pitfalls of legalism. One of the passages, in fact, the first one that I'm going to share is so important that the author of the book of Hebrews actually quotes this Old Testament passage in detail. The passage is found in the prophecies of Jeremiah, where the Lord says:

> ***"Behold, the days are coming, declares the Lord, when I will make a new covenant with the house of Israel and the house of Judah, not like the covenant that I made with their fathers on the day when I took them by the hand to bring them out of the land of Egypt, my covenant that they broke, though I was their husband, declares the Lord." Jeremiah 31:31-33***

What do you see in this passage? Understanding, first of all, that these statements were made during the time Israel was under the Mosaic Covenant, let's highlight the key statements.

The first thing God tells us through Jeremiah is that **He's going to make a new covenant**.

The second thing He says, is that ***it will not be like the covenant I made with their fathers***. It's critical that you see that.

So, when did this "new covenant" become activated? Luke records Jesus' words during the Last Supper, saying:

> ***"This cup that is poured out for you is the new covenant in my blood." Luke 22:20***

There it is! Jesus inaugurated the new covenant *during* the Last Supper. And just like the Old Covenant, it was established through the shedding of blood. But this time, it was the blood of the innocent Savior.

Once again, God revealed through the prophet Jeremiah that the New Covenant would be *"not like"* the old one. And yet, for 2,000 years Christians have been trying to merge the Old Covenant with the New. Whether it's Sabbath days, food restrictions, feast celebrations — we keep trying to fill old wine-skins with new wine!

What happens when you do that? You get Christianity plus law-keeping. Sure, you can be a Christian, but you have to go to church on a special day. Yes, you can be a follower of Jesus, but you have to avoid eating certain foods. It's Christianity with rules and laws heaped on top and it's an absolute mess!

No!! God said the New Covenant would be *different*. And the Lord reveals that difference a little later in that same prophecy from Jeremiah:

> ***"...For this is the covenant that I will make with the house of Israel after those days, declares the Lord: I will put my law within them, and I will write it on their hearts..." Jeremiah 31:33***

Did you catch that? One primary difference with the new covenant is that God will take His Law and write it on the hearts of His people.

This is referring to the coming of the Holy Spirit. Think about it!! The Law Giver — the very One who gave the Law to Moses and to Israel **now lives within us** and His Law is now written on our hearts. That means the Law is now *internal*. We no longer need to be guided by an external law written on tablets of stone. The Law is now inside you — it is written on your heart and on your mind.

A Living Law

A good way to think about this is to compare it to the laws that we have in the United States. Many of those laws are posted on signs for all to see, but none of those signs live inside of you — they're all external to you. As you're driving along the road, you see a speed limit sign on a street or highway, and that sign tells you that you may go as fast as the posted limit and no faster. If you decide to exceed the posted limit you will end up breaking the law.

Now, imagine you're driving along with no smartphone or GPS to tell you the speed limit which means you're totally unaware of how fast you should go until you actually come upon a speed limit sign. You're driving along thinking, *'Gee, I hope I'm not driving too fast.'*

Finally you see the sign telling you the speed limit for the road you're on. The problem is, you had to wait until you saw the sign. You were guessing right up to that point because not every state has the same speed limit. Although our neighboring state of Idaho allows speeds of 80 miles per hour on the freeway, when you get to my home state of Oregon, the speed limit drops down to 70. But until you see the speed limit sign, you wouldn't know that because the law of Oregon is *external* to you.

But wait, what if those signs weren't necessary? What if technology, (and this sounds a little scary, but bear with me) had a way of taking all the laws of the land and putting them *inside our hearts?* We wouldn't need signs anymore because the moment you cross a state line you would instantly know what the speed limit was because it was ***inside of you***.

This is precisely what has happened now that you've received the indwelling Holy Spirit. You don't need an external law telling you not to commit adultery or not to steal or lie because now it's all right there in your heart! That once external law of God is now alive and speaking within your heart — communicating His will and His desire for your life. God has made obsolete the old, external tablets of stone by replacing them with His very Spirit.

"The law giver now lives *within* us."

Please don't think I am minimizing the Law or saying we shouldn't care about it anymore. I care very deeply about it because the Law has now become one with my desire. This is what the Apostle Paul meant when He wrote:

> *"...it is God who works in you, both to will and to work for his good pleasure." Philippians 2:13*

So, how should we now view the Old Testament Law? A passage that answers this for believers is found in Galatians chapter three where the Apostle Paul wrote:

> *"...the law was our guardian until Christ came, in order that we might be justified by faith. But now that faith has come, <u>we are no longer under a guardian</u>." Galatians 3:24-25*

Paul tells us the Law was given "**as a guardian**." The Greek word refers to a *tutor* or a *trainer*. But the Apostle writes, **'now that faith has come'** I don't need that same guardian anymore. He has given me something far superior to my old tutor — He has given me *Himself!*

Some final thoughts...

I can imagine this chapter might be challenging for some. You may need to read through it again. But the Jews living in the first century definitely found this message challenging and many accused the Apostle Paul of preaching a message that would only end up subverting the Law of God and a law-abiding civilization along with it. They believed Paul's teaching would result in disorder and lawlessness. That is why he put forth this question:

> *"Do we then overthrow the law by this faith? By no means! On the contrary, we uphold the law."*
> **Romans 3:31**

Paul understood that some would strongly object to his teaching about faith apart from works of the law. They would say that he was flagrantly dismissing the demands of God's holy righteous standards. But Paul insisted that the opposite was and is true — faith actually *enables* people to uphold the law because the Holy Spirit first communicates the will of God to the redeemed heart and then He enables the believer to live accordingly.

These insights concerning your relationship to the Law are safeguards to help you to rightly understand your relationship to the law. And such safeguards are vital because you are now prepared for that well-meaning Christian who says, *'You've got to do it this way'*, as they point to one of the external laws from the Old Covenant. But you can look them in the eye and say, *"I have the Law Giver living in my heart."*

Dear Josh,

As uncomfortable as this revelation may have been for you, I think the Lord brought Julie into your life to make you aware that the joy and assurance we have in Jesus has nothing to do with keeping rules, but is instead based solely on the finished work of Jesus on the cross. It's apparent to me that you already see the error of legalistic thinking and the Lord has made you aware of the futility of earning God's favor by the keeping of rules. What remains is for you to walk out this newfound freedom in Jesus and to serve the Lord with your whole heart — not because you must but because your heart is overflowing with thanks and gratitude for what Jesus has completed on your behalf.

Blessings to you in Jesus,
Pastor Paul

Chapter 4
Because the enemy has convinced you of things that aren't true

I imagine I could write an entire book outlining all the ways Satan can negatively influence believers, but in this chapter I want to focus on exposing three lies perpetuated by the enemy that are most often used to lure believers toward feeling that God has become distant. Those lies are:

- You've sinned to the point that you can no longer be forgiven

- You've blasphemed and committed the unpardonable sin

- You will never be free from the sin that holds you captive

Dear Pastor Paul,

Thank you for always taking my emails. Even though we don't go to your church, my husband and I listen to you online.

I really appreciate how you always remind everyone that we cannot earn salvation by our works. It is something I need to hear a lot! But I still struggle having confidence in my salvation. I pray but something inside me just refuses to accept that Jesus died for me personally.

I know Jesus died for the sins of the world and whoever comes to him he will not cast out, but, I have sinned so much! Some days I feel like I've stepped over the line.

The other day someone told me that doubting your salvation is a way of blaspheming the Holy Spirit. Is that true? Can I truly be forgiven? I am so messed up. Please help.

Amanda

***

Jesus made it clear that Satan is a liar and the **"father of lies." (John 8:44)** To be the father of something is the Bible's way of saying Satan is the originator of lies and deception. The enemy masterfully exploits our human weaknesses like a pro, knowing just where to attack. He is vicious and merciless and his goal is to get you to believe that God has moved on and left you behind and alone.

In the following pages, I will address each of these three lies and also share the powerful tools that God has given to His children to not only combat the enemy but to be more than conquerors.

Lie #1: You've sinned beyond God's forgiveness

What do you see when you read the letter from Amanda? I see a work of the enemy that has caused a condition of double-mindedness. Did you notice Amanda wrote on the one hand: *"I know he died for the sins of the world and whoever comes to him he will never cast out..."* And then, practically with the same breath, she goes on to say: *"Some days I feel like I've stepped over the line."*

Those statements together reveal contradictory thoughts swirling around in her heart. On the one hand she knows that Jesus suffered to bear her sin, but on the other hand she is so aware of her own past failures that she can't seem to let them go. Because of that, she now doubts whether she is truly forgiven.

And that is precisely where Satan wants to keep your focus — believing that your problem (sin) is bigger than the solution (the sacrifice of Jesus on the cross). Satan knows that keeping you fixated on your sinful past will keep you paralyzed, full of doubt, and filled with the nagging fear that you've been abandoned by God.

The reason this lie of the enemy is so effective is because Christians lose sight of the fact that our salvation has nothing whatsoever to do with our sinful past. Jesus died to erase that past and to secure our complete forgiveness. Satan can't change what Jesus did, so he does what he *can* do, which is to get believers to doubt their forgiveness by directing their focus onto their sin instead of on Jesus and the cross.

The battleground for these believers is the mind — a mind that must be renewed in the absolute truth of God's Word to the point that you realize your sinful past cannot ruin what Jesus did for you. And the only way that's going to happen is if you focus your attention on the truth of God's Word and learn to resist the temptations of the enemy to look back and ponder the depravity of your past.

Remember this, looking at *self* is *always* counterproductive. Keeping your focus on Jesus and what He did on the cross brings peace and joy.

The tools for walking in victory are these:

Confession. Go before the Lord and confess your failure to keep your eyes on Jesus and ask the Lord to forgive you for focusing on the sin that He has already forgiven.

Pick up that shield. It is vital that you take up the shield of faith with which you can extinguish the flaming arrows (lies) of the enemy. *(See Ephesians 6:16)* This shield is made up of our faith in God's wonderful promises concerning His love and forgiveness.

Have confidence. Commit to memory the promise contained in **1 John 1:9** and raise it as a shield whenever the enemy tempts you to look inward.

Lie #2: You've blasphemed and committed the unpardonable sin

Please don't be offended when I say that Satan preys on human ignorance. When someone tells me they are absolutely certain they have blasphemed God to the point that they have committed the unpardonable sin, I know I'm dealing with a wounded heart and an insufficient understanding that is now being exploited by the evil one.

This is a classic case of misunderstanding the Word of God. The two passages that most often create fear issues are Matthew 12 where Jesus addresses the sin of blasphemy against the Holy Spirit and Hebrews 6 where the author of that book discusses those for whom repentance is no longer possible.

I have found that both passages along with the definition of what constitutes blasphemy is woefully misunderstood.

First of all, in Matthew chapter 12, Jesus defines blasphemy against the Holy Spirit as attributing a miracle performed by Jesus through the power of the Holy Spirit to the power of Satan.

Blasphemy is something that originates in a heart of unbelief and hatred toward God. It cannot be committed by accident or in a sudden outburst of emotion.

> "Keeping your focus on *Jesus* and what he did on the cross brings *peace* and *joy*."

And there are many, myself included, who wonder out loud if blasphemy against the Holy Spirit is even possible anymore, since

Jesus' explanation of what constitutes that type of act seems to require circumstances that were unique to the time of His public ministry.

Hebrews 6, on the other hand, was written to Jewish Christians who, due to persecution and fear, were being tempted to return to the Law of Moses as a means of being justified before God. The author explained that there is no possibility of salvation under those circumstances. And yet, the statements in Hebrews 6:4-6 continue to be taken out of context and exploited by the enemy causing tender-hearted believers to think that because they've back-slidden they cannot return to the Lord and are now condemned to an eternity in hell.

Nothing could be further from the truth!

The key to not getting tripped up by either of these passages lies in *understanding their context* and taking care not to pull single verses or statements away from the overall meaning of the passage, thereby allowing yourself to become unsettled.

Satan is tireless in his accusations and condemnations of believers, but the Lord Himself declares:

> ***"The steadfast love of the LORD never ceases; his mercies never come to an end; they are new every morning; great is your faithfulness." Lamentations 3:22–23***

Christians who are laboring under the weight of the enemy's attacks need to begin to believe that God's mercy is greater than their ability to sin. As the Apostle Paul wrote: ***"where sin increased, grace abounded all the more." (See Romans 5:20)***

Lie #3: You will never be free from the sin that holds you captive

Behind the smile of many born-again believers there's a silent war being waged with the enemy over some kind of sin from which they seem to be unable to break free. And because they fall to this sin from time to time, Satan is quick to rush in with a hopeless message, telling them they are slaves of sin and however hard they may try, they will never be free from its grip.

Because they have believed the lie of the enemy they now feel dirty and unworthy of God's love and attention. This causes them to feel hypocritical about reading their Bible or praying or going to church. It all comes together to form a perfect storm of discouragement and depression that only emphasizes the distance they feel from God.

I will readily admit that there are some sinful habits that seem more challenging to overcome than others. But the Bible tells us that God has given us *"everything we need for life and godliness." (2 Peter 1:3 NIV84)* At some point every believer needs to understand that the power of the cross and what Jesus accomplished there is greater than the power of sin to dominate your life. Jesus truly is able to secure the victory over our sinful flesh. The key is not allowing yourself to give up. Believers need to be patient and let the Lord do His work of cleansing and renewal.

When I encounter a Christian who has fallen prey to this lie of the enemy, I encourage them to do a deep dive into the sixth chapter of Paul's letter to the Romans. There are passages there that powerfully explain the plan of God to set the child of God free from the power and grip of sin. One beloved brother of mine even took it upon himself to memorize that incredible chapter and it had a profound impact on his life and brought a freedom from sin that he had sought for many years.

Note: My own study in Romans can be found at: **lifebibleministry.com/romans** or by taking a photo of the code below.

One final thought...

God's Word wants you to know this about Satan — *you can resist him*. Peter writes:

> *"Your adversary the devil prowls around like a roaring lion, seeking someone to devour. Resist him, firm in your faith..." 1 Peter 5:8-9*

Please understand, dear believer, that apart from Jesus you have *no ability* to resist the enemy. He is so much more powerful than you, but he is *not* more powerful than your Father in Heaven. You have the Lord of life living inside you through the Holy Spirit, and through His indwelling presence you now have the power to resist the devil. But this requires that you be *firm in your faith*. In other words, resist him *as* you stand firm in the promises of God. You can do that. You can say *no*. You can pray against the work of the enemy. You can pray for God's protection. You can *stand* against all the lies that would otherwise cause you to feel estranged from God.

These are the biblical keys that will keep you on course as it relates to your life in Christ as you stand safely behind the shield of faith.

My dear Amanda,

Jesus died to save sinners and promises that if we will come to Him with sincere and believing hearts, we will be cleansed from ALL sin. He suffered terribly on the cross to pay the penalty of your sin and mine and when that price was paid He boldly announced, "It is finished!" The work has been done and there is nothing left but to believe and receive. Stand fast in the love of your Savior and recite His promises whenever your heart is heavy.

Remember, dear sister, there is therefore now no condemnation for those who are in Christ Jesus.

Blessings to you,
Pastor Paul

Chapter 5
Because living in a broken world has shaken your faith

I don't believe it's an overstatement to say that the majority of emails and letters that I receive come from believers who are distressed by the painful and agonizing realities of living in a fallen world. Brokenness dominates our world, our homes, our bodies and our minds. It can easily become overwhelming and notes like what follows are commonplace.

Hi Pastor Paul,

My name is Peter and my wife and I have been following your messages online for quite some time now. We are both believers and have been involved in our local fellowship doing various things. Recently my wife's health has deteriorated and now she has been diagnosed with a life threatening disease which we're told could end her life within a couple of years.

The two things I have learned from the Bible are: 1) God is not obliged to provide answers and rarely does; and 2) the fact that God is sovereign means that His will is the final determination in all things. That leaves me with the conclusion that my wife is suffering because God wants her to suffer.

Are there any other answers? I don't see any.

Regards, Peter

***

Getting notes from believers who are suffering severe hardships are, quite frankly, hard to read because I can always sense a heavy weight of discouragement.

I get it. As I write this chapter my own wife is undergoing treatments for breast cancer and experiencing all the terrible side effects of chemotherapy. Over the years I have seen my share of people suffering and have stood by silently when words of comfort and consolation simply weren't sufficient enough.

Rains, Floods, Winds

In His Sermon on the Mount, Jesus used a parable to illustrate the difficulty of living in this world. He began by using the imagery of a house being built on one of two foundations. The house is a picture of our lives. He went on to describe the things that come against that house saying, **"the rain fell, and the floods came, and the winds** *blew and beat on that house..." (Matthew 7:27)* Obviously, these are metaphors for all the painful and distressing things that can happen to a person. At yet another time, Jesus abandoned all metaphors and pointedly declared, *"In this world you will have trouble." (John 16:33 NIV84)* And the Apostles would often tell the believers, *"We must go through many hardships to enter the kingdom of God." (Acts 14:22 NIV84)*

All of these passages help us to understand that God's Word both recognizes and warns us of the dangers and heartaches associated with living in a fallen world. In the blink of an eye our lives can go from joy to tragedy, comfort to hurt and satisfaction to deep disappointment.

And yet, there is a danger that surpasses the challenges of this world and that danger is the way we respond to the worst that this fallen world can dish out.

I have personally watched believers respond to hurts and troubles with disappointment and anger and I have also seen them respond with faith and confidence. Each response bears its own unique fruit. One draws the child of God ever closer to their Lord and the other makes Him seem a million miles away.

To all who have been touched by this fallen world and felt the sting of personal hurt and loss, I share the following important reminders from the Word of God.

Reminder #1. This world isn't heaven. Not even close. We dwell in a sin-soaked, fallen and corrupted place where things go wrong every single day. Life on planet earth is a constant challenge with pitfalls and dangers all around. The fact that we have *any* good days and experience any happiness at all is only because of the mercy of God.

In **Romans 8:20–23**, the Apostle Paul used phrases to describe this world, such as: *"subjected to futility"* and *"bondage to corruption"* and *"groaning...in the pains of childbirth"*. He went on to describe we, who are children of God, as those who "***groan inwardly***" as we daily witness the corruption and deterioration of society. Paul referred to all that we endure as *"**the sufferings of this present time**." (Romans 8:18)*

Reminder #2. Everything we see — all the pain, all the corruption and everything we suffer — is a constant reminder of why God sent His Son to earth. Jesus came because the world and those who inhabit it are irreparably broken and the coming of our Lord signaled the beginning of God's plan to redeem mankind and overturn the terrible effects of Adam's great failure.

Because God has shared his master plan with us, we now know that all we see will one day be made new. This is why believers "**groan inwardly**" — we long to see all things renewed and we know our suffering will not be in vain.

Reminder #3. Jesus has overcome the world. We cannot remind ourselves of this truth too often. Jesus conquered death and the grave. Yes, we will experience death if the Lord tarries in His coming, but, to enlarge on the passage partially quoted in the previous reminder, the Apostle Paul wanted us to know that our current sufferings, "**are not worth comparing**" to what awaits us when Christ returns. This is why Jesus told us to, *"...**take heart; I have overcome the world**." (John 16:33)*

Reminder #4. We will be profoundly affected by whatever we fix our eyes upon. This is a truth that we must know and understand. We were never told in God's Word to fix our eyes on the troubles and sufferings of this life and yet that is exactly what we do and the result is what the Bible calls *losing heart*.

Peter well understood this idea of keeping his eyes on Jesus. He was the disciple who, during a terrible storm on the Sea of Galilee, dared to ask Jesus that he might step out of the boat and come to His Lord walking on the water. The Bible tells us that Peter actually did just that, until something stole his attention: **when he saw the wind, he was afraid (Matthew 14:30).** It was at that moment that Peter began to sink. And the same thing happens to each and every one of us as we turn our attention away from Jesus and focus instead on the hurts and troubles of this world.

Thankfully, Peter had the good sense to cry out, **"Lord, save me."** Peter's actions provide for us such a powerful picture of where our attention ought to be. We can either fix our eyes on the fact that we are **outwardly...wasting away** or we can fix our eyes on the inward renewal of our hearts. When we do this, suddenly the sufferings of this life take on an entirely different perspective. We begin to see them as **light and momentary troubles** that are actually working in our favor to bring about **an eternal glory**.

This is exactly what the Apostle Paul explained in **2 Corinthians 4:16–18** where he said:

> *"So we do not lose heart. Though our outer self is wasting away, our inner self is being renewed day by day. For this light momentary affliction is preparing for us an eternal glory beyond all comparison, as we look not to the things that are seen but to the things that are unseen. For the things that are seen are transient, but the things that are unseen are eternal."*

Never forget that a fixation on this world produces disappointment and discouragement. But keeping our eyes on Jesus produces hope and **"hope does not disappoint us." (Romans 5:5 NIV84)**

Convinced of God's Love

When troubles arise, our enemy will be quick to suggest that God has withdrawn His love and attention from your life. He knows that painful circumstances make that a fairly easy suggestion to make. But that's precisely why the Apostle Paul wrote about the depth of God's love for us — even in the midst of struggles and pain to which Paul was no stranger. In Romans 8:38-39 he actually made a list of the things that are powerless to dampen or nullify God's love for us. That list includes: death, life, angels, demons, the present, the future, powers, height, depth, or anything else in all creation. ***(Cited from Romans 8:38-39)***

You have to admit, that list pretty much covers it all. And concerning all those things, Paul wrote, "***I am convinced...***" The Greek word means *to be persuaded, to be confident, to trust*.

Are you convinced (persuaded and confident) of God's love even when life is hard, or does your heart become an easy target for the lies of the enemy during seasons of hardship? If your honest answer is anything less than complete confidence, I encourage you to come before the throne of grace and confess this lack to Jesus. Ask Him to do a work in your heart that will convince you beyond all doubt of His overarching love for you.

> "...and we *know* that for those who love God *all* things work together for good..."

Waiting is Hard

WHY DO I FEEL SO DISTANT FROM GOD?

I remember several years ago McDonalds ran a promotion claiming that if you didn't get your food handed to you within two minutes, it would be free. I actually recall seeing a digital timer in the drive up lane that counted down those two minutes. I don't recall how long that promotion lasted but it certainly played into society's craving for instant gratification.

Waiting is hard and I've never been a fan. But when you take waiting and add troubles and hardships on top of it, it is misery itself. Even worse, take waiting and hardships and then throw in an unknown outcome and life quickly becomes unbearable.

People suffer for all kinds of reasons. There's suffering involved for simply being a follower of Jesus, which is seen as honorable and even biblically desirable. There's suffering due to poor choices and bad decisions. And then there's suffering that comes simply from living in a fallen world, such as when someone becomes sick or is the victim of an accident. Such situations happen to all of us and it is then that we must learn to patiently endure.

I truly believe one of the reasons the enemy finds such a ready and inviting environment in our hearts to convince us that God is distant is because we have failed to grasp what the Bible has to say about patiently enduring hardships. It's far too easy to skip over passages that speak on this topic. Nowhere are these truths more beautifully communicated than in John's powerful introduction in the first chapter of Revelation. Just the first several words of verse nine are what A.W. Tozer referred to as ***an ocean of truth in a drop of speech***.

> ***"I, John, your brother and partner in the tribulation and the kingdom and the patient endurance that are in Jesus..." Revelation 1:9***

The year was AD95 and John was on the island of Patmos in the Aegean Sea. This was no vacation destination. It was a penal colony used by the empire to confine and isolate the enemies of Rome. John had fallen into disfavor with Emperor Domitian for preaching the Gospel of Jesus Christ and testifying to all he had seen and heard. His suffering was real and ongoing. And yet, John considered it all part of **the tribulation and...patient endurance that are in Jesus**.

To patiently endure simply means to wait for troubles to end. Trouble can be defined as the presence of something bad or the absence of something good. But for believers, the culmination of our waiting is for a Person. The Psalmist said it best: **"I wait for the LORD, my soul waits, and in his word I hope..." (Psalm 130:5)**

To wait is not simply to accept the passing of time. For we who are in Christ, waiting is an act of *faith* — a determination to trust that the Lord knows our pain and will take hold of our troubles and afflictions and use them for His purpose — the purpose for which they were allowed in the first place.

This is patient endurance and the working of it keeps us from giving in to the lies of the enemy seeking to convince us that God is distant and indifferent to our concerns and fears.

To swallow those lies is to invite anger, frustration and bitterness. To hold fast to patient endurance is to invite peace, hope and —this is the strange one — *joy!*

How strange the Apostle Paul's words must have seemed to the believers in Philippi, knowing that he had written them

from a Roman prison when he said things like, **"Rejoice in the Lord always; again I will say, rejoice." (Philippians 4:4)**

But Paul meant those words because he understood what it was to patiently endure in hope. Listen to what he wrote to the Church in Rome:

"...we rejoice in our sufferings, knowing that suffering produces endurance, and endurance produces character, and character produces hope, and hope does not put us to shame, because God's love has been poured into our hearts through the Holy Spirit who has been given to us." Romans 5:3–5

As the Scripture says, **"Anyone who trusts in him will never be put to shame." Romans 10:11 NIV84**

> "For we who are in *Christ*, waiting is an act of *faith*."

Dear Peter,

I feel the weight of your discouraged heart, so let me quickly remind you of God's firm love and tender concern for you and your dear wife. He has promised never to leave nor forsake us and I am convinced that one day we will see that He has kept that promise. During times of difficulty and challenge, I encourage you to stay closely connected to God's Word and to bring your wounded and heavy heart to the Lord in prayer. Follow the lead of the Psalmist who cried out to the Lord holding nothing back. My friend, God knows all that you have suffered and He longs for you to surrender it all at His feet. His promise is that He will never abandon or forsake you. He actually challenges us to trust Him with *all* of our hearts. *Bring it all to Him and find solace for your soul in His comforting presence.*

Your brother and companion in the suffering...that are ours in Jesus...
Pastor Paul

Chapter 6
A Final Word

If you could only know the metamorphosis this little book went through from its inception to final completion. It's probably the closest thing I'll ever experience to childbirth, complete with pushing and moments of panic.

It all started with a teaching I shared on a Sunday morning in 2023 titled, **Biblical Keys to Staying on Course.** I knew there was something special about that message and I felt the Lord prompting me to lay it out in book form. But that basic outline went through a lot of incremental changes until I eventually changed the title.

I have encountered *so many people* over the past several years who have expressed similar symptoms of feeling distanced from God that I knew it was more than a fluke. As I read between the lines of each and every piece of correspondence I came to realize that the enemy had been hard at work spreading his lies and half-truths to the point that people were falling hard into his deceptions.

None of the letters in this short book are exactly as I received them, but were reworded in such a way as to reflect the intent and experiences of real people with whom I have corresponded. The names were changed but the stories and experiences are as genuine and raw as they come.

My intention in sharing the challenges of God's people is to contradict one of the most effective weapons of the enemy, which is to make believers think they are the only ones struggling, while the rest of the Body of Christ enjoys constant and unbroken intimacy with God. Nothing could be further from the truth.

And while it is certainly comforting to know that we are not the only ones who struggle, my larger goal has been to expose common ways believers fall prey to wrong thinking and offer the kind of biblical help that can enable them to make a life-changing course correction.

As a Bible teacher, I have become increasingly convinced throughout my years in ministry of the incredible effectiveness of the Word of God and its ability to transform a life when it is mingled with a humble and teachable spirit that chooses to submit to the Living God. And yet, the very Scripture that declares itself to be "living and active" is too often set aside and ignored by the very ones who would confess it to be the inspired and written Word of God.

But I have seen what happens when believers take what they know to be true about the Bible and begin to walk it out in their daily lives. Suddenly the message of the Bible becomes personal and applicable. The heart of the believer swells with acceptance and joy as they begin to take in the Word as personalized communication from their Father in heaven and they are filled with hope and life.

It is this that enables us to navigate and overcome the challenges that we face in this life. As Jesus said, "***I have told you these things, so that in me you may have peace. In this world you will have trouble. But take heart! I have overcome the world.***"[1] The very Word of God that we consume on a daily basis empowers us to take heart amidst all the brokenness and chaos of a sin-filled world. It also

---

1. John 16:33 (NIV84)

strengthens us against the many deceptive lies of the evil one that attempt to get us to despair and wander off course.

Dear saint, do not forsake the Word in your life. It is your lifeline and the very nourishment of your soul.

Pastor Paul LeBoutillier

> "Do not forsake the Word in your life. It is your *lifeline* and the very nourishment of your *soul*."

About the author

Paul and Sue LeBoutillier have pastored Calvary Chapel Ontario for almost 35 years. The Lord has allowed Pastor Paul's verse-by-verse Bible teachings to have a world-wide audience through Youtube. Sue has many women's Bible studies both written and video series through Women of the Word.

This is Pastor Paul's second book. His first, *Pastor, I have a Question*, can be found on Amazon or through the link below.

Visit **lifebibleministry.com** or take a photo of the code below.

Made in the USA
Middletown, DE
05 March 2025